Wabi-Sabi

Perfect imperfections

Shalini Gupta

BookLeaf Publishing

India | USA | UK

Made with ❤ on the BookLeaf Publishing Platform
www.bookleafpub.in
www.bookleafpub.com

Dedication

To Maam sir...words will never be enough to express my
gratitude.
Mummy and Papa... Thank you for being my greatest
cheerleaders.

Preface

This book is truly a labour of love. Many poems from the collection are from personal experiences. Some of these were written on demand and a few by chance.
I am eternally grateful to family and friends who keep on encouraging me and give me ample reasons to put my thoughts into words.

Acknowledgements

When you manifest, it happens! Ialways dreamt of holding my published work in my hand and it's coming true!
Thank you @blueleafpub.in for making it happen for dreamers like me.

1. Life and death

With each death I die
wonder if life is just a lie,
a corpse lying tells a story
either happy or sorry,
life betrays
death embraces,
then why to cry
when a near one dies!
why to hold grudges and fight
when we can love and be light.

2. Smile

Smile when you're alone
smile when you're in a group,
smile when there are friends around
smile when silence makes a sound,
smile when you are weary and tired
smile when there isn't any reason for it
smile not for the sake of it,
smile not to fake anything
smile.. because it's your way of life
smile because you take everything in your stride,
smile because you own your thoughts
smile because of the inner battles you have fought,
smile to spread your light
smile.. because it gives delight.

3. Random Thoughts

Randomly my life goes
there are no friends or foes,
I take life as it comes
sometimes it surprises me
sometimes I succumb,
for all the unhappy moments when I am sad
there are these moments which say..
' life is not that bad!'
my garden is abound with beautiful trees
they abode chirruping birds and buzzing bees,
marigold, hibiscus and jasmine
spread happiness which was still unseen,
screeching squirrels dig the ground
to hide seeds in leaps and bounds ,
I ruminate and realise
in random things beauty lies.

4. Amma

The ever warming smile
the eyes that love your sight
the hands that hold yours,to confirm
that it's you,
the intimate hug and a million blessings..
it was a regular thing whenever
I came to meet you Amma,
you passed away on the date I came on earth
you died when we became very close,
when we started to share time with each other,
you are gone but only physically,
spiritually you are always there,
a guardian angel who protects
me from evil spirits
a mute, unseen friend, whom I speak
to ,with my mouth shut,
whenever I feel being lucky
whenever things are going in my favour,
i know you are showering your love and blessings
from up there!

5. Karvachauth

I keep this fast for your long life
as I am a dutiful wife,
At the crack of dawn
I take 'sargai' with a yawn,
Throughout the day, I wait for the night,
A glimpse of the moon,
My fast would be a feast soon!
sometimes I ponder and ask myself
who keeps the fast, you or I?
Everyday you fast..
fast for the office
fast for the deadlines
fast for meetings and greetings,
fast in fulfilling our demands
fast for your future plans,
fast in connecting the dots of our life.
everything you do, is with a fast pace,
with always a smile on your face.
Amidst all this, I think again

of the moon at night,
'coz, I am a dutiful wife..right?

6. Nearing Fifty

As I am nearing fifty
I fear my impending death,
not as I am fearful of dying
but because I have just started living!
Till now I was a daughter, a wife and a mother
now I am for myself beyond others.
I have desires, even if a few,
I made a bucket list too!
Hindustani classical I want to learn,
my own money, I hope to earn.
I seek crochet as a new hobby,
A published writer I aspire to be,
My dreams aren't castles in the air
I simply wish a life, beautiful and fair.

7. I am yet to be discovered

As I am in class twelfth
physics, chemistry and mathematics are now my wealth,
I take pride in increasing my knowledge
but sweat profusely when I think about college!
my elders see an engineer in me
my friends say " a techie you'll be!"
I love to be in uniform
and aspire to be a soldier ,
at times I wonder how will it be
if I become a professor!
My journey is not a race ..
let me walk on my own pace,
I am still a caterpillar, yet to be butterfly
let me discover my horizons and fly high.

8. It's okay to be mediocre

there are no pins and medallions on my blazer
my mind is not as sharp as a razor,
I am what I am
I learn, I make mistakes,
I am laid back many a times
but now I work diligently
as now is the time,
my future is performance based
I have tightened my reins
I am paced,
I will keep working better and better
day or night, now will not matter,
I am better than yesterday
I will be better than today,
I will not rest
till I become the best!

9. You and I

Through thick and thin
come rain or shine
you are there by my side
a helping hand
my best friend
you brighten my day
in a very special way
I made a wish
you came true
some call it love
I call it you!

10. Teenage

Teenage looks chirpy and charming
It seems full of dreams,
A stage when one there is a change all around
A phase when actions and voice seem profound ,
If you cry , you are called a baby
If you advice , you are named matured,
Life becomes upending, a torture for sure!
What one sees is a rebel
What one ignores is lovelorn being,
Detachment is not the way out
Communication is the key.

11. Complications of the mind

I wish to weave a pattern of thoughts
A tapestry of words.
My innermost feelings
Entangled in my head
Urge to be shaped by my hand.
The pleasure of writing is entwined
With the complications of the mind,
So much I aspire to express
My heart is in constant distress.
To navigate my wavering thoughts
I just scribble and jot.
Will these conversations ever blossom
Will I be able to craft a poem?

12. Fragility of life

How fragile is life
how futile our ways become,
how do we accept death
even when we are aware
that it will come!
it breaks families
it shatters dreams,
no amount of tears help
nothingness seeps.
we heal with time
but superficially,
The heart doesn't heal.
Tears dry up,
sympathy piles up,
we are weird beings..
we come back to our routine .
In retrospect, one ponders..
what mattered was the person,
who is now resting in peace

Not the things, which
were accumulated piece by piece!

13. In Search of Myself

Who am I?
A mother..a sister or a wife ?
A friend..a daughter or a loner in strife ?
I still don't know who am I!

May be a juggler or a pedlar
Or I might be a nomad
who belongs to nowhere
but is seen everywhere!
one who does multitasking for survival
but still remains an individual!

why am I sad of being alone
I must be happy in the company of my own!

My only best friend is me
nobody understands me better than me!
after giving so much to others
I realise, nobody bothers!

Now my priorities are set
I am a different person, you bet!
whatever I have lost in between
will be gained if
I become a Mr.Bean!

14. FaceTime

Sometimes a FaceTime is more than a video call,
you swipe up to see a familiar face
A heartwarming smile greets you
you are teary eyed too!
The phone is then twirled around
Many happy faces, boundless happiness now surround!
Salutations and flying kisses pour
to take you to a roller coaster childhood tour,
Nostalgia fills the air
Alas! With some despair!
We cousins are not separated
we are just scattered
whatsapp binds us together!
I'm so upbeat for that FaceTime
I realise I am worth someone's time.

15. Menopause

Change is a constant with everyone
It touches all , spares none
I feel some drastic changes
in my body and mood
I am mostly bloated and often rude!
I frequently cry for no reason
I sweat a lot in winter season!
Face I look at in the mirror gives me pain
Life now seems mundane!
"This too shall pass" , I tell myself
sometime soon, I will be my usual self,
In the mirror I now see a beautiful reflection
I tell her softly...
"Buck up gorgeous girl
Sing, dance and twirl
Its Me-No-Pause
not Menopause!".

16. On Mummy's 70th birthday

How should I wish you
When all your wishes are a blessing to me,
What can I gift you
When my existence is a gift from you,
How can I make your 70th special
When you have given me infinite special moments,
Those who know you…
Know love better.
You smile, you laugh, you sing and you dance
With life as your suitor, you romance!
May I be as loving and caring as you
Perhaps that would be my gift to you!

17. Nostalgia

Walking down the memory lane
Is like holding a best-seller,
A myriad feelings are stored
Waiting patiently to be read.
Each memory is a chapter,
Some make you laugh, some give you joy
The most emphatic makes you cry!
You want to hold the moment forever
But it slips before long,
Nostalgia is a melancholic song!
However staggering the the past was
Its gone forever,
It can never be recreated
For worse or for better.

18. Ferris wheel

'Have a nice day!' I said
While waving at them,
They responded by smiling
And waving back to me.
Everything is same
The father, the car, and the kid,
Everything is different
The father, the car, and the kid.
Earlier, the innocent eyes
Would be teary-eyed
While leaving for the play school,
Now, experienced eyes
Have tears of joy
As 'the kid' accompanies him to the office.
Life is an amusement park
It never fails to entertain,
Each experience is a joyride
Exciting moments it contains.
Just like a Ferris wheel
It makes a full circle,

Role reversal gives goosebumps
And that makes it awesome!

19. Photo albums

This poem needs some introduction. I have a great collection of photo albums. Not the digital one, but the real one.

My children have tried their level best to school me about the convenience of maintaining digital albums and here is my reason for keeping the hard-covered photo albums:

Dear Arnav and Avishi

When you grow up and I grow old
Life will turn many a fold,
I will not be the same as now
Let me tell you how,
With weak eyes and failing ears,
With hollowed cheeks and a wrinkled face,
My frailed body will not let me stand straight!
Then, these albums in my hand
Will work like a magic wand.
Our life is a rainbow,

We have our sunshine and rains
These albums will make me smile
And take away the pain.
These are my private literature
Which I will cherish forever.

20. Three magical words

'I love you'
makes our life a worth,
'I miss you'
reassures us,
'See you soon'
is extremely comforting,
'Get well soon'
tells somebody is caring,
'God bless you'
gives divine warmth,
'Please, sorry, thank you!'
shows how graceful we are!
These magical words
from time to time
makes our day
soothing and sublime.

21. Happiness

Happiness is a state of mind
It is the way of life,
It doesn't depend upon what we have
It depends upon what we can provide.
when jealousy and selfishness is everywhere to be found
Impact of happiness is deep and profound.
It doesn't need any validation and explanation
it just requires empathy, friendliness and compassion.
Happiness keeps our innocence alive
It keeps us healthy throughout our life.